T0147080

A TRUE STORY

*Of Our Lord and Savior, Jesus Christ
and His Never-ending Love*

S H I R L E Y   L O G I E   P E R R Y

WESTBOW
PRESS®
A DIVISION OF THOMAS NELSON
& ZONDERVAN

WestBow Press books may be ordered through booksellers or by contacting:

WestBow Press
A Division of Thomas Nelson & Zondervan
1663 Liberty Drive
Bloomington, IN 47403
www.westbowpress.com
844-714-3454

Scripture quotations taken from The Holy Bible, New International Version® NIV® Copyright © 1973 1978 1984 2011 by Biblica, Inc. TM. Used by permission. All rights reserved worldwide.

ISBN: 978-1-6642-6697-1 (sc)
ISBN: 978-1-6642-6696-4 (e)

Print information available on the last page.

WestBow Press rev. date: 05/13/2022

"I lift up my eyes to the hills –
Where does my help come from?
My help comes from the Lord,
The Maker of heaven and earth."

Psalm 121, 1-2
New International Version

CONTENTS

INTRODUCTION

Good Lord willing, this memoir will be submitted for publication before my passing. I leave these memories to my children, Cynthia Ann Reuber (nee Gropp) and Darren James Gropp. I wish for them to give a copy to each of my grandchildren, so they may understand how our Heavenly Father has led me throughout my life and how He never abandoned me from the day that I was born, not even through the many years that I lived in sin and darkness. It is my testimony that the Lord was always there for me, with me, even during the darkest times of my life, even when I did not realize that He was there. He was and is guiding me.

I believe that I was placed on Earth to help lead others to the Father, Son and Holy Ghost by helping the poor, the suffering, and the needy. Simply stated, I believe my purpose is to humbly serve the Lord and help lead others to Him.

Memories are illusive and individual. Everyone has a slightly different recollection of a shared event. This memoir is accurate as I recall to the best of my human abilities.

CHAPTER
One

My earliest memory is that of me as a toddler. We lived on the second floor of a small country store in Milverton, Ontario. My parents owned and operated the store to earn a very meager living. I remember climbing up and down the steep steel steps on the outside of the building at the back of the store.

I remember when I was very young (not sure how old I was at the time), that our parents would go out to the local hotel to drink and get drunk, leaving myself, my two younger sisters and my brother alone. We didn't realize where our parents were at the time, but were told by others about our parents' frequent hotel trips later in life.

Sarah Ebersol, a very dear Christian spinster lady, lived across the road from the store. I know that she was a Mennonite lady because she wore a white bonnet and dressed in long, plain gowns. I believe she was an Old Order Mennonite. She was our guardian angel. When our parents would leave us alone, Sarah would come over, sneak in to watch over us until our parents returned. Then she would sneak back out through the back steps and go home, so Mom and Dad wouldn't know that she had been there.

Looking back, I realize that Sarah was sent by God. Without her, we may not have survived childhood.

Later, we moved into town. My parents managed to get a house in town. It was a small frame wartime house with two small bedrooms upstairs. We three sisters slept in one bedroom and our brother, Lavern (he preferred to be called Bert after our father) slept in the other bedroom.

The bedrooms were heated with a metal stovepipe that was connected to the pot-bellied woodstove in the living room below. The stovepipe then made a 90-degree angle in our brother's room, crossed the connecting hall, then extended through our room to the chimney.

The stovepipe would get very hot, and we had to be careful not to get too close to it. I remember worrying about the room catching fire while we slept.

Our father had a mortgage for $2,000. That was the total price for the house. It took him almost his whole life to pay for it because he worked in a furniture factory for 50 cents an hour. Where he really got the money to pay off the mortgage was when my step-brother (from Dad's first marriage), Walter, passed away from brain cancer at the age of 42. Dad took Walter's life insurance which was $2,000.

I say "took" because that is literally what he did. The actual life insurance beneficiary was my step-sister, Audrey (from the same marriage). My father took her to court, sued for the money, and the judge awarded it to him.

Dad was always abusive to his children from both marriages. Ironically, Walter's brain tumor was probably linked to the many beatings he (like all of us) endured, having his head kicked too many times when he was a little boy.

I remember being tied to the potty chair as a toddler, sitting there and crying to get off because the plastic potty seat was hurting my very tender skin.

My mother would ignore me and just keep working in the store.

It made me feel so very unimportant and unloved.

Another early memory dates back to when I began school. I was 7 years old before I was permitted to go. My parents held me back a year so that I would be starting school with my sister who was a year younger than me. I was to help her because as my mother repeatedly told us, "Gladys was a blue baby." Never understood what that meant, but we were never to upset her. She wasn't allowed to participate in any physical exercises, not even in school.

When I was in grade 3 (I would have been about 10 years old), my mother left our father. She had a boyfriend take her and her four children to a city several miles away from Milverton. She then placed each of us in a different foster home. She rationalized that, if Dad came looking for us, he would be looking for a woman with four children. In reality, she was probably motivated by a more selfish and less cunning reason to "farm out" her children. As an added bonus, Mom didn't have to be a mom for about a year at least.

Eventually, she decided it was time to go back to Milverton and Dad.

I recall that I was the last one of her children to be picked up from the foster home.

Again, unimportant and unloved.

CHAPTER
Two

M om worked as a nurse's aide at the Milverton nursing home, not far from where we lived, taking care of the elderly. Back then one didn't need any education or special training to work as a nurses' aide. Mom took great pride in working there; in fact, for the rest of her life, she would call herself a nurse.

One night, Dad came home from the hotel and said to me, "Go downstairs and bring up a pail of coal." It was for the coal stove that we used to heat the house. So, being afraid of him, I did, but when I brought it upstairs, he bellowed, "I told you to bring up a pail of coal, not a level pail of coal. You didn't heap it up!" The coal was very heavy for a fifteen-year-old to carry up from the basement, and I was very frail, tall, and skinny for my age.

He hated me.

Dad began to beat me and kicked me down onto the floor. He kicked my head against the sharp edge of the wooden vanity in the kitchen that housed the oblong badly-dented metal sink and the pump, the only source of running water in our home. I managed to get up and briefly escape. I ran into the next room, the living room. Big mistake!

The living room was next to our parents' bedroom. He caught me, threw me down onto their bed, and continued to beat me. He laid his huge body down on me and beat my head from side to side again, and again, and again, until I was nearly beaten to death! He got up, and I managed to get away again. I ran back into the kitchen.

I ran straight to the knife drawer and grabbed the biggest butcher knife we had, the kind of knife that butchers use to carve meat and slice through bone. I was trembling and afraid for my life, so trembling that I had difficulty holding the huge knife. In spite of my great fear, I found the strength to hold it straight up in front of me.

"Come and get me,!" I screamed. "I will shove this knife right through your big, fat gut!"

He was slowly, menacingly approaching me. My eyes were fixed on his fat, beer-bloated, watermelon belly. But then I looked up and saw my brother, Lavern, sneaking up behind Dad. Lavern had been listening to everything that was going on from his bedroom upstairs. He was big like Dad, and he grabbed him from behind and held both of Dad's arms to stop him from coming any closer.

Lavern yelled, "Run, Shirley, and don't ever come back!" I fled through the kitchen door and ran like the wind, shaking and trembling all the way. I ran all the way to the nursing home and asked for my mother. I told my mother what had happened.

Looking back, I recall that Mom did not seem at all surprised.

All Mom said was, "Do you know anybody in town that would allow you to spend the night?" and "I will come to see you in the morning."

I told her, "Yes." I had met a boy close to my age, David Edgar, and he seemed quite nice.

That is how I ended up meeting the Edgar family. I went there trembling so hard I could barely breath and asked if I could please spend the night to hide from my father. They said, "Yes, of course!" All night long, I remember sitting there, trembling and shaking.

CHAPTER Three

The next morning, Mom showed up. She told me that she had put my two younger sisters on a passenger train. Their destination was a place I had never heard of before, Glencoe. Why there, I am not sure. She had gotten her pay from the nursing home and only had enough money for two tickets, so she let the two youngest go by train. Mom and I were to hitchhike. The plan was to be in Glencoe in time to meet the train.

Mom and I grabbed a few -- very few -- belongings and took off walking out of town carrying our meager belongings. All through the night, we walked and tried to get somebody, anybody, to stop and give us a ride.

Finally, a transport truck stopped and let us get in the cab with him. I don't know what Mom told him, but I heard him say, "If you will leave me alone with your daughter, I will take you all the way."

Mom just sat there as though she was actually thinking about it, so I spoke up and said, "Mom! Really?"

After an agonizing silence, Mom finally said, "No."

Looking back, now that I am much older, I realize that Mom must have been absolutely desperate.

So, the truckdriver pulled over to the shoulder of the road, stopped, and said, "Get out!" We did.

We went back to hitchhiking and managed to get another ride. Thankfully we made it to the train station in Glencoe in time to greet my two sisters.

CHAPTER
Four

From there, we went to live with a man who had lost his wife and needed a housekeeper. Mother had gotten the job.

He lived a short distance out of town in a very old farmhouse with several bedrooms. Mom stayed there with my sisters and I stayed in Glencoe by myself. She got me a room at the town's only hotel.

The hotel put me in a huge, basically empty room that had been used years earlier as their bridal suite. But it was empty because they hadn't rented it in years, so they rented it to me. There was an army cot to serve as my bed and a white porcelain sink on the wall so I could wash my hands. There was a washroom a long way down the hall where I could use the facilities or take a shower. I had no clothes to hang up, so I didn't need a closet. I remember having a bedcover that I used for a blanket.

There didn't seem to be anyone else staying there. I never saw anyone. It was not only lonely but quite scary for me.

Mom explained, "If your father comes looking for us, he will be looking for a woman with three girls. If you stay here, there will only be a woman with two girls." Also, because I was staying in town, I would be able to get a job." Then she left.

Even though I was only fifteen, I did manage to get hired at a local factory where they made socks. At the time that the twister sock, a special ribbed sock very popular with teenagers, was the in-fashion. I was hired to sew the fringe around the top of the socks on a sewing machine.

I hadn't even gotten my first pay yet when my mother came to see me in my huge, empty room. Mom announced that she and my sisters were going back to Dad. I was to stay in Glencoe to fend for myself. Dad was coming to pick them up the next day. She was only there to say, "Goodbye." I wasn't given the chance to say goodbye to my sisters.

The hotel owner was there, and she said, "I'll leave you alone to say goodbye." She probably thought there would be an emotional moment between my mother and me.

On the contrary, Mom's cold, emotionless response was that anything she had to say to me, she could say in front of anyone. She left me with a two-dollar bill. My first payday was still two weeks away. She took off her watch and gave it to me. With that, she closed the door behind her. I remember throwing the watch on the floor and stomping on it. That was how I felt about that.

Realizing that my family had left me there all alone, I took my two dollars and went to the store in search of something to eat. Things were much less expensive in those days. I bought a loaf of bread, a jar of sandwich spread and one bar of Dove soap so I could take a shower. I had no way to refrigerate my sandwich spread, so I kept it on the window sill between the storm window pane and the inside window pane. Luckily, Canada's weather provided natural refrigeration.

I continued to work in the factory. Time spent in my big, empty room was very lonesome, so I took a second job to occupy more of my time. After working in the sock factory each week-day, I also worked evenings and weekends at the town's restaurant where I waited on tables and ran the cash register. They let me have a little to eat, but I was afraid to ask because I was a new employee, and I didn't even know them.

Because I was so young and living at the hotel, I

was afraid to walk back to my big, empty room at night. Each night, the hotel owner's husband would walk me home.

I continued to work both jobs for a while. Then, one night, I went home to bed and slept for about two days. When I didn't show up for work on the second day, they came to check on me. They found me passed out from starvation and took me immediately to the doctor.

After that, it seemed that everyone was offering me food. The girls at work brought me a food basket. The hotel owner offered me meals in their dining room, and they allowed me to run a tab and just add it on with my rent.

It was hard for me to make friends because nobody knew me. They only knew that I lived at the hotel. I would be alone at night and cry and cry myself to sleep. If anyone knocked on my door, I would pretend that I wasn't there because I was afraid.

Looking back, I am sure that I must have been extremely depressed.

CHAPTER
Five

One particularly lonely night, when I was missing having a family, I was close to a total breakdown. I phoned my mother and asked if I could come home. She asked Dad and he said, "Yes," so they came and got me.

For a while, things were good. That was when I met and began dating the man who would become my first husband, John.

I got another sewing job in a factory in Stratford, just seventeen miles up the road, and I commuted with a Milverton man who also worked in the same factory. I earned enough to pay room and board to my parents, the agreement made with them when I was allowed to move back home.

My life seemed to be going in the right direction, to have a purpose.

Then the ticking bomb exploded. I learned that, while I was living in Glencoe, my father in one of his nightly drinking binges at the local hotel had gotten up on top of a table and announced to everyone there that the reason we had all left him was because I was pregnant and needed to leave home.

God only knows that, if that was true, I would have lost the baby the night he kicked me in the stomach while wearing his Army boots.

I guess I knew then what everyone in town would think of me. What could I do about it? Nothing. Not if I wanted to stay home.

Because of what happened next, I think that someone in town told Dad that I was telling a different story about what had happened and how badly he had beaten me.

It happened on a Saturday afternoon. I was upstairs with my sisters in the bedroom when I heard my mother calling me to come downstairs.

Mom was waiting for me at the back door to the house. She said, "Your father and I are going to Hanover for the day. When we get back, we want you gone. And

I don't mean just your dad; I want you gone too!" She never gave me any reason, not then or ever.

I asked, "Where have I got to go?"

She calmly and coldly said, "I don't know, but you'd better be gone."

I hadn't been dating John long enough to ask him for help. However, when my stepsister, Audrey, heard the news, she and her husband, Bill, offered to let me live with them. She said, "We have a brand-new house with an extra bedroom. You can move in with us."

I did, and they were very nice to me. Since I still had my job in Stratford, I earned enough to pay Audrey and Bill for room and board; however, I still could not afford to get my own apartment. Besides, I didn't have any furniture.

The Lord must have been with me that day. I don't know what I would have done if Audrey and Bill had not offered me a place to stay.

I stayed with them for a few months, not sure how long. It was hard for me knowing that I had family just a few blocks away but I wasn't welcome there, not even for a brief visit.

One afternoon, when I was downtown, I saw my mother and she would not even look at me! I was so upset about that. When I told Audrey, she had me lay down and put my feet up. She was kind to me. Audrey knew what my mother was like.

CHAPTER
Six

John and I were still seeing each other, but one afternoon my brother, Lavern, came to see me. He asked me if I would like to go to London with him to visit the Edgars, the family who had allowed me to stay with them the night my father had beaten me so badly. Lavern said that he would bring me back to Audrey and Bill's house that night.

I was just pleased to hear from anyone in my family, so I happily agreed to go with him. Unfortunately, he did not bring me back that night. Lavern didn't return home until the following day.

I was afraid that, if I went back to Milverton then, John would break up with me because I stayed overnight at the Edgars' home. John was suspiciously jealous of the Edgar's son, David. John, I feared, would think that I had gone to see David and not to see the Edgar family. John had a nasty temper.

David asked me to stay. Being young and foolish, I agreed to stay with the Edgars because I didn't feel like I had any reason to go back to Milverton.

Big mistake! I didn't bother to ask the Edgars if I could stay. Unfortunately for me, I was not welcome there, and they tried everything they could to get rid of me, short of just saying, "Get out!"

Instead, they tried getting me a job on the other side of the city. (Milverton is a small town, and I had never learned how to take a bus since I never needed one to get across town.) The job was a factory job sewing bathing suits, but I needed to take a bus to get there.

The first day on the job, David went with me to help me get there. I loved my new job. It seemed easy, and I was good at it.

Then it was time to go home. I think that I may have gotten on the right bus, but I certainly didn't get off at the right place. There I was, lost in the city. I couldn't even remember the right address; maybe they never gaveit to me.

I was certainly naïve, a country mouse lost in the big city, so I walked and walked looking for a familiar street. I was so lost! (I knew at that point that I never would be able to keep that good job.)

As night fell and it grew dark, I grew more tired and more afraid with each step. Eventually, I saw a police officer and told him about my being lost. I didn't even know the address where I was staying.

The officer managed to find their address just by their names, and he took me home.

I don't think they were glad to see me back because I didn't even know how to take a bus. I knew then that they didn't want me, but I didn't know what to do.

I recall that they would all eat supper together at the kitchen table, but they never asked me to join them. They could see me watching them eat, but they never gave me anything. I was always hungry.

Then they helped me find a job babysitting, and the lady that I babysat for told me that I could eat anything I wanted. Her family was Catholic and I wasn't. They tried taking me to church with them, but it was all in Latin and I couldn't understand a word or know what to do. There I was again, another big disappointment.

By this time, David had started making advances toward me. I thought that, if he loved me, he would help me. Being the fool that I was, I started having an affair with him. Another big mistake! Two months later, guess what? I was pregnant!

No. The Edgars did not accept it. They tried everything they could to get me to lose the baby. His mother told David to take me on very long walks, maybe even try to get me to lift the washing machine. I was desperate, so I finally did something.

When my next payday came from babysitting, instead of the Edgars taking me home, I told them that I had called a cab to go downtown shopping and would take a cab home later.

Actually, what I had done was call my mother. Once again, I asked if I could come back home even though I knew they didn't want me either. To my surprise, she said, "Yes." She told me to go to the train station and catch a ride to Milverton. She said, "Your father will pick you up at the train station."

I called the train station and asked when the next train to Milverton was leaving. In a short while, I was on the train and, for a brief while, I felt free.

I remember that it was in the fall, and it was very cold. All I had on was a cheap cotton sundress.

When I arrived in Milverton, my father met my train. He said very little to me, but he took me home. My parents had company ("church" company – apparently my parents found religion while I was gone), and I guess they were ashamed of me. They hustled me quickly upstairs to the bedroom and out of their sight. They didn't want their church friends to see me so poor and undernourished.

But I was happy just to be back home, for all that was worth.

The next day, I told my mother that I was pregnant and that David did not want the baby or me. She said, "I was afraid of that." Mom took me to a doctor. I thought she wanted to make sure that I was alright. But it wasn't for assurance at all.

The doctor gave me some pills to take and said, "If you don't start to bleed within three days, well then I guess you're going to be a mother."

But then I did it. I took the pills, miscarried, and was taken to the hospital.

During my hospital stay, the only available reading material was a Bible supplied by the Gideons. I now see this as a "God wink" intervention.

I later lied about the reason for my hospitalization, telling people that I had been in the hospital for malnutrition. In those days, a woman was very frowned upon if she had a child out of wedlock.

It wasn't long before John saw me walking to the store in downtown Milverton. The old, familiar feelings returned for both of us, and soon we were "back in love" with each other. Marriage offered me the hope of a "real home," so when he proposed, I accepted. We were married a short time later.

CHAPTER
Seven

John always made me feel like he was disappointed with me. He had a job working as a meat inspector for the government, and I did not even have a grade 8 education. In fact, I had been promoted to each succeeding grade level because of my age, so I didn't feel that I earned the grades. The teacher once told me that he knew my parents were going to make me quit school the day I turned 16, and he wanted me to have "at least grade 8." My birthday in March of that year insured that I would not complete the year; thus, no grade 8.

(The same fate came to my sister Gladys. Our parents made her drop out the day she turned 16, so she didn't qualify for the "good jobs" either. She and I have always gotten along very well, and she has always been my favourite sister.)

Years later, Gladys and I both ended up living in Aurora, Ontario. Gladys lived temporarily with me and John. John always insisted that I have a job outside of the house, but because of my lack of formal education, the "better" jobs were unavailable to me.

When my son was about 4 weeks old, John announced that he had found me a "wonderful opportunity" to go through training for a dental assistant. Gladys took on the babysitting duties for me so I could take advantage of this wonderful opportunity.

One day at work, I heard a baby crying in the waiting room, and it upset me. For some strange reason, the crying made my breasts hurt. I didn't know why until it was time for me to quit for the day. The crying baby was my son, Darren, and since he was still breast-fed, instinctively his crying made my breasts hurt. Subconsciously, my body knew that the crying infant was my baby.

When I returned home, I called back and quit the job. I knew that I needed to be with my son.

John was angry with me that I gave up the "wonderful opportunity" to better myself. I never measured up to my great meat inspector husband.

Marriage between equals is difficult enough, but marriage between unequals is an exercise in futility.

My marriage to John ended in disaster! Before we even brought up the subject of divorce, he cheated on me. John found someone better suited to his lofty standards, and literally threw me to the curb! The view "from the curb" was familiar territory for me; it was just another hurdle for me to overcome.

Looking back, I now realize that John thought that I wasn't "good enough" for him, but God knew that I needed to "exit" this toxic marriage. I believe that God had already chosen someone much better suited to me, someone who needed me as much as I needed him.

Exit John.

Enter Tom.

CHAPTER
Eight

I met Tom Perry at a singles' dance at a time in my life when I was feeling very alone and rejected because I knew that my first husband had already found someone else John had made it very clear to me that he wanted me out of his life. He had moved on with his life. After 27 years of marriage and at 47 years of age, I was not accustomed to being single.

Tom is a very quiet man, a nice surprise, compared to the bombastic, condescending John. Tom is a good listener and very kind to me. It wasn't long before we became very close.

He had grown up on a farm and was accustomed to working very hard. When he was still very young, he saved up his money and purchased a truck. He became a trucker, hauling cattle and later vegetables, etc. That was probably what prompted him to open a store. In a short time, he owned 4 stores and was managing them himself. He has always worked very hard.

I really needed a change in my life and was ready to make it. When he offered to help me open a store of my own and teach me to manage it, I accepted his offer. I was hoping to erase some of my past and move forward with my life.

Tom also had a failed marriage in his past, and his first wife had remarried. After about a year, Tom and I married, and I moved my store in with one of his in Wingham, Ontario. After the Wingham store closed, I returned to work as a cook in a local hotel kitchen.

We have now celebrated 27 years of marriage and are retired. We were forced to retire early because of Tom's health problems; he has battled serious health issues for several years. I have endured my own serious health issues at various times through the years.

We have a very good marriage and have always been good to each other. Tom has never raised a hand to me, fought with me, or abused me in any way.

I believe that the Lord knew that I could not endure any more abuse in my life. I am trusting Him to help me through and give me strength to bear whatever lies in my future. Life can be hard and cruel, but I have faith that Jesus will help me overcome.

Tom always lets me know that I am loved, needed and wanted. He has given my life stability, at last, after a lifetime of being forced out of my home and having to start all over again. It has happened to me so many times, that some people secretly referred to me as "the bag lady!" I carried all my belongings in black garbage bags and seemed to be always looking for a place to call home. Yes indeed, I became very good at making a fast get-away and making a fresh start. As the adage says, "What doesn't kill you makes you stronger."

My "stay" strength has always been the love I feel for my two children that the Lord blessed me with from my first marriage. Cindy, my daughter, and Darren, my son, gave me a family of my own to love. I learned from the miserable life I had before Tom, that I could never allow anyone to abuse my children! My children have given me a lot of strength through some extremely trying times.

My children have had a very difficult time growing up in an unstable home, a home with no shortage of turmoil between their parents. I deeply regret that I was unable to be a stay-at-home mom with my children when they needed me. I always had to have a paying job to provide them with food and other necessities.

With a lot of help from above, as long as the Lord allows, I will always be there for them. They have both given their lives to Christ. Cindy has blessed me with 4 grandchildren AND 4 great-grandchildren. They have all accepted Christ. I am truly blessed!

CONCLUSION

I believe that Jesus wants me to profess His love to the world – this world full of turmoil, hatred, shamefulness, all manner of wickedness, racisms, and prejudices—to free those who are imprisoned by sin. I was afraid that I would not be able to see this writing through fruition for several reasons:

- my lifelong habit of attempting to do 3 or more things at a time;
- the damage done to my brain by my father's recurring beatings while my brain was not yet completely formed;
- my advancing age;
- and my health challenges.

But I am trusting in the Lord to help me because I believe that He wants me to record my life's journey.

I recently celebrated my joy in the Lord with a small house party. Guests included my precious children

(Cynthia and Darren), my loving husband (Tom), and a very dear longtime friend (Kathleen). She is my "sister in Christ." Kathleen is now 95 years young. I am truly blessed.

I have been struggling to turn my atheist husband to Jesus for years now. When I was at the Dollar Store, I picked him up a T-shirt with the words "Jesus Loves this Guy" on it. He wears it for me every time I ask him to wear it. Praise you, Jesus.

I would like to conclude by saying this.

> **If Jesus blesses you with a gift, don't refuse it or give it away. He wants you to have it for a purpose. It is all part of His plan for your life.**
>
> **Always keep your eyes toward the heavens; don't look down in despair. That's where the evil one lives. He will surely not help. Evil will destroy you.**
>
> **All things work for good if you are serving God. When I think of all the things I have been through, I consider my relationship with our Heavenly Father to be paramount! He has always been there to pick me up, assure me, and bring me through life's trials. However hard the trials seem to be, difficult places often lead to beautiful places.**

He loves to give good gifts to those who serve Him and obey His commandments. Nothing is too hard for the Lord.

There are always flowers for those who want to see them. Shoot for the stars. Nothing is too far!

I am loosely paraphrasing one of my favourite Bible verses:

There is a time to be born, a time to cry,
a time to wonder why,
a time to pray, a time to ask and watch,
a time to begin, and a time to die."

God bless you!

Printed in the United States
by Baker & Taylor Publisher Services